Wynn-Anne Rossi

Once There Was a Boy

Notes from the Publisher

Composers in Focus is a series of original piano collections celebrating the creative artistry of contemporary composers. It is through the work of these composers that the piano teaching repertoire is enlarged and enhanced.

It is my hope that students, teachers, and all others who experience this music will be enriched and inspired.

Frank J. Hackinson, Publisher

Notes from the Composer

Inspired by and dedicated to my own son, Nicholas, these pieces are designed to celebrate the particular way in which a ten-year-old boy experiences the world around him. Like many others, Nick fits in quite well with the classic images of boys his age. His fantasy is being a space alien, and his reality is the world of worms and discovery. One thing is obvious: he thoroughly enjoys being a boy!

Wynn-Anne Rossi

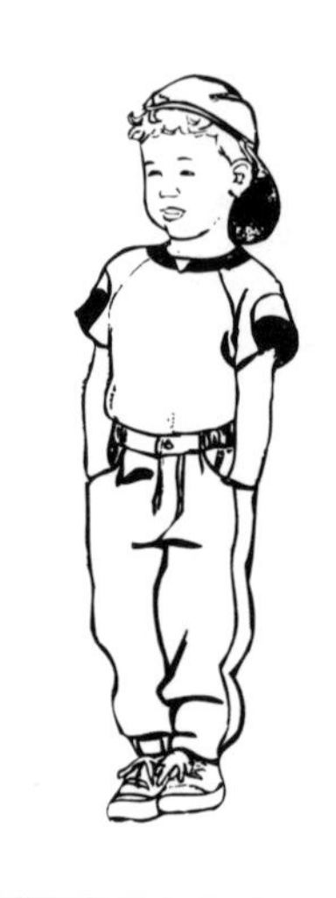

Contents

Mud Pies

Mischievously ♩ = ca. 132
Wynn-Anne Rossi
Stick - y and oo - ey and mes - sy and goo - ey, and
mp
is - n't it glo - ri - ous? I feel vic - to - ri - ous.
Some think it's yuck - y when they get all muck - y, but
mud is a mar - ve - lous thing!
Teacher Duet: (Student plays 1 octave higher)
p

17
Think of the tur - tles and the worms,
mf
21
hav - ing a won - der - ful time;
25
Dig - ging and turn - ing, ooz - ing and gooz - ing,
29
get - ting all cov - ered with slime!
f

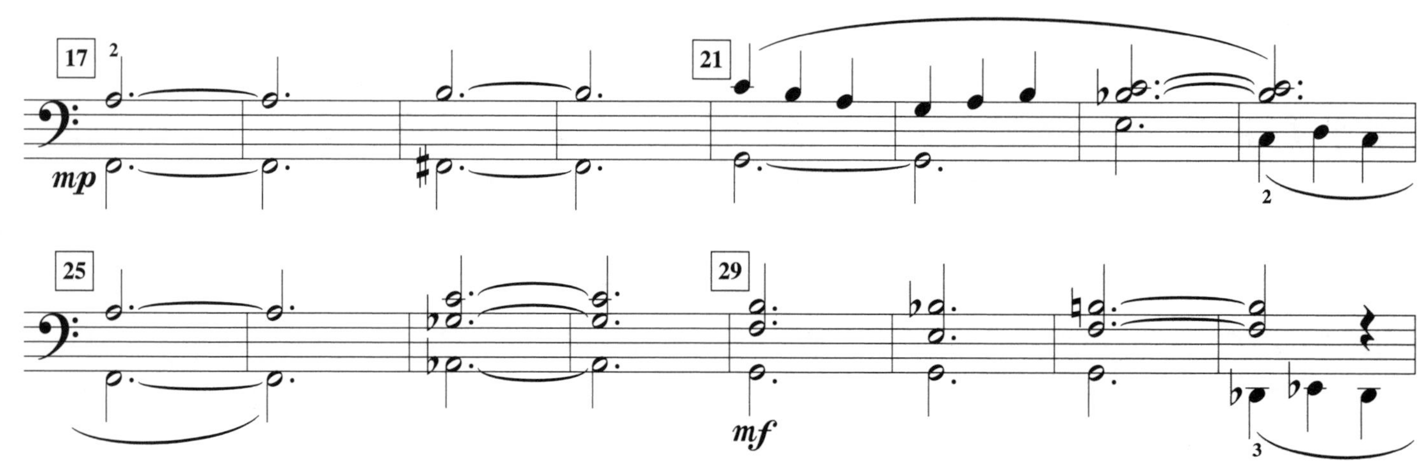
17
mp
21
25
29
mf

33
Stick - y and oo - ey and mes - sy and goo - ey, and
mp
37
mak - ing mud pies makes a ver - y fine day. It's the
41
best game I know that I ev - er can play,
poco rit.
45
a tempo
uck - ing and muck - ing in mud!
f
33
p
37
41
poco rit.
45
a tempo
mf

Puppydog Tails

Happily ♩ = ca. 156
mf
Frogs and snails and pup - py - dog tails,
Frogs and snails and pup - py - dog tails,
5
pok - ing a hor - net hive;
mak - ing me feel a - live.
9
Wig - gle - y things, squig - gle - y things, some - bod - y
p
mp
14
get my but - ter - fly net!
Teacher Duet: (Student plays 1 octave higher)
mp
5
9
pp
p
14

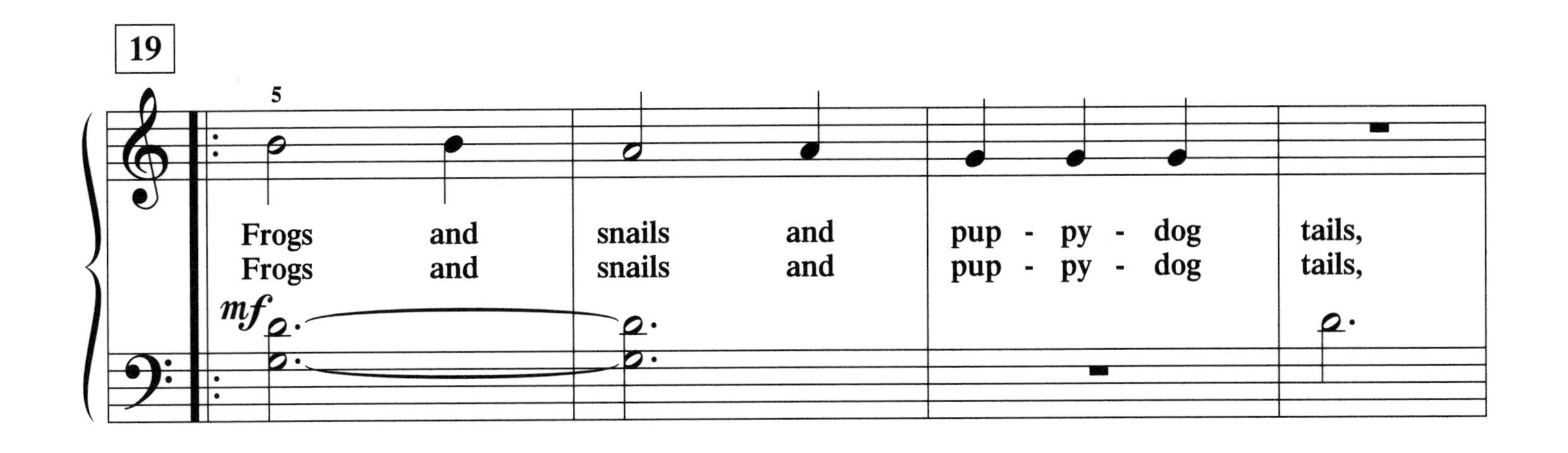
19
5
Frogs and snails and pup - py - dog tails,
Frogs and snails and pup - py - dog tails,
mf

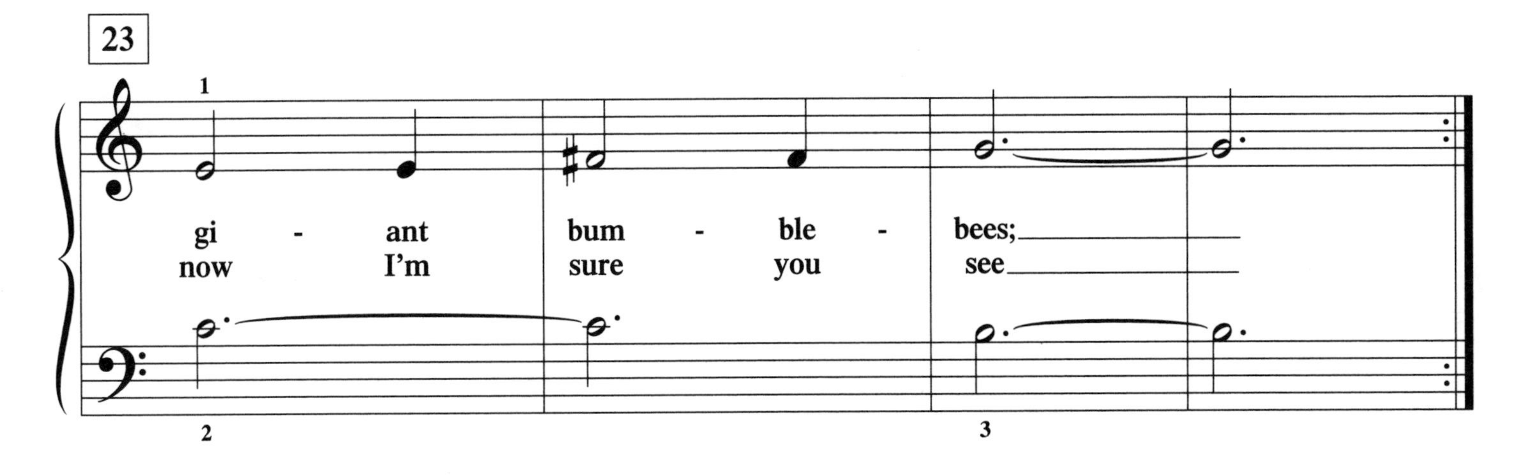
23
1
gi - ant bum - ble - bees;
now I'm sure you see
2
3

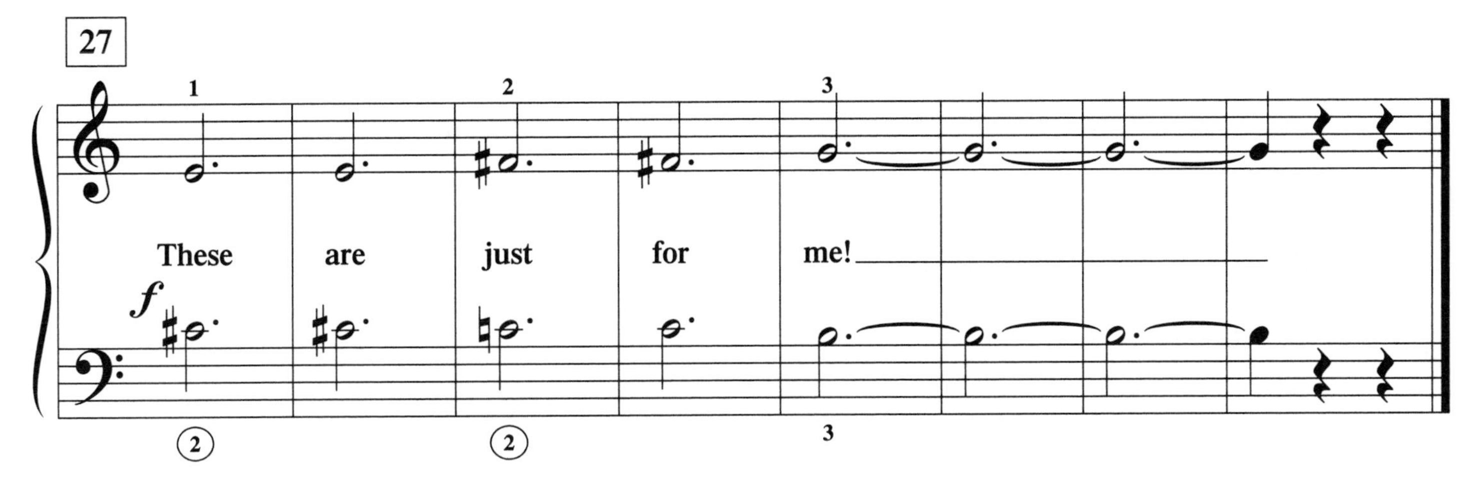
27
1
2
3
These are just for me!
f
2
2
3

19
5
23
mp
27
mf

Computer Whiz

Precisely ♩ = ca. 172

Teacher Duet: (Student plays 1 octave higher)

17
Ed - it it!
Fi - le it!
Make a print!
mf
21
Play - in' com - pu - ter is fun!
25
Ma - ma says I'm bril - liant, so I nod and smile;
29
a tempo
Push de - lete...
Uh - oh! It's gone!
f
17
mp
21
25
29
a tempo
mf

Raptor Rumble

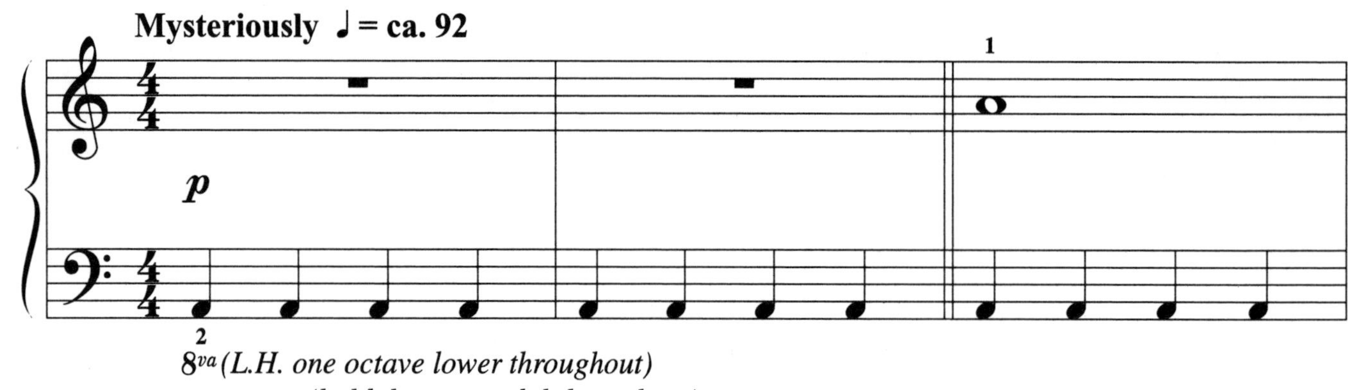

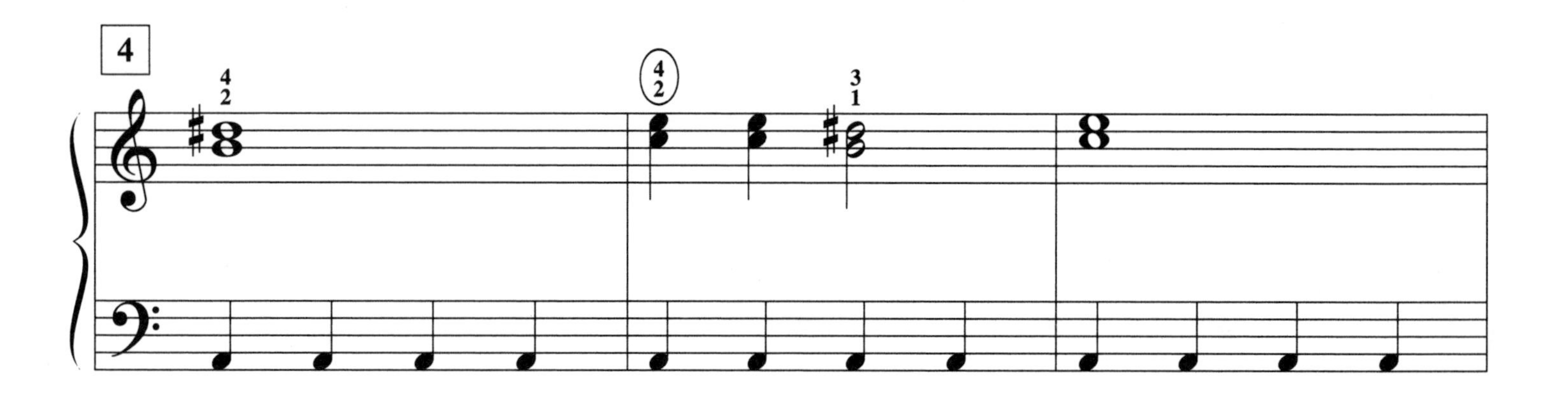

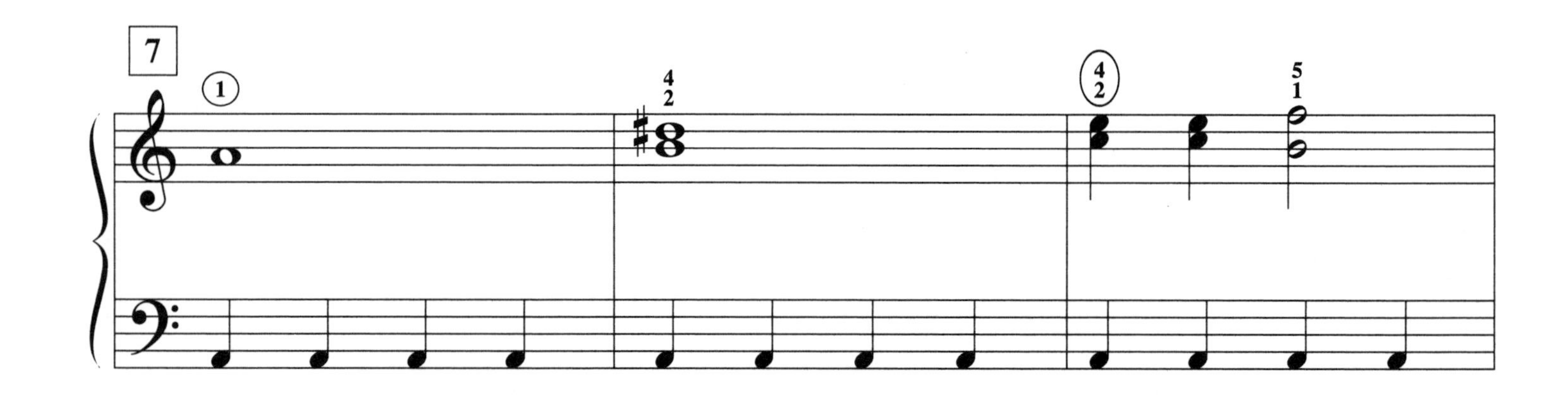

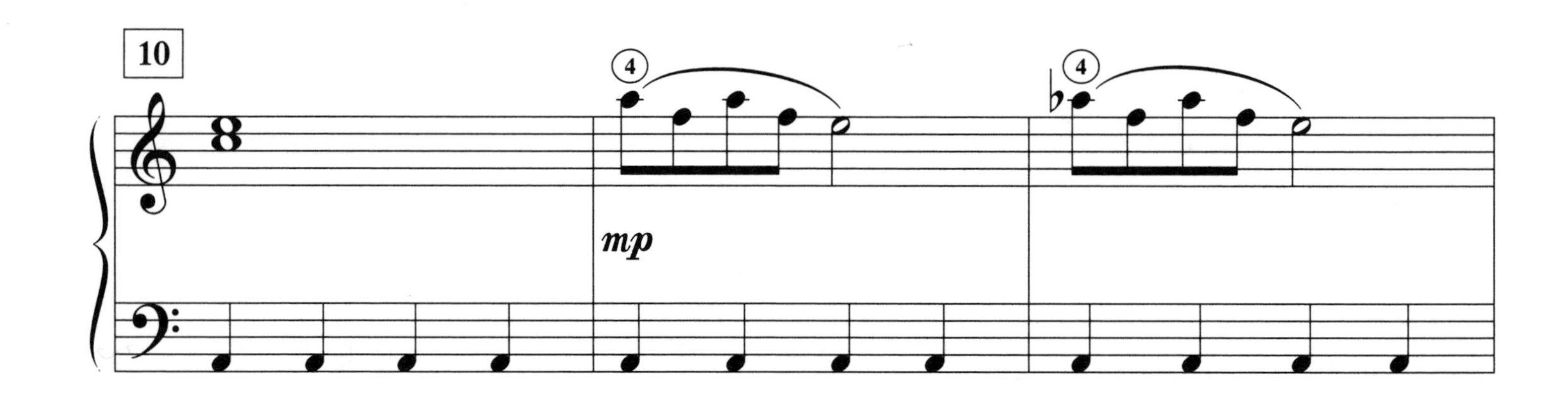

13
mf
16
cross over
19
p
22
25
Slower
poco rit.

Clean My Room???

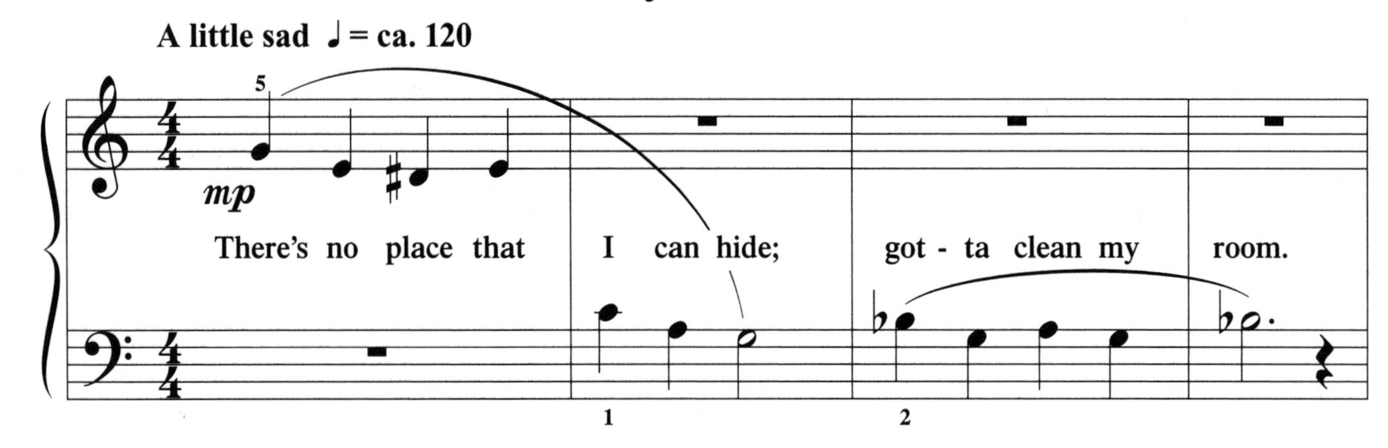

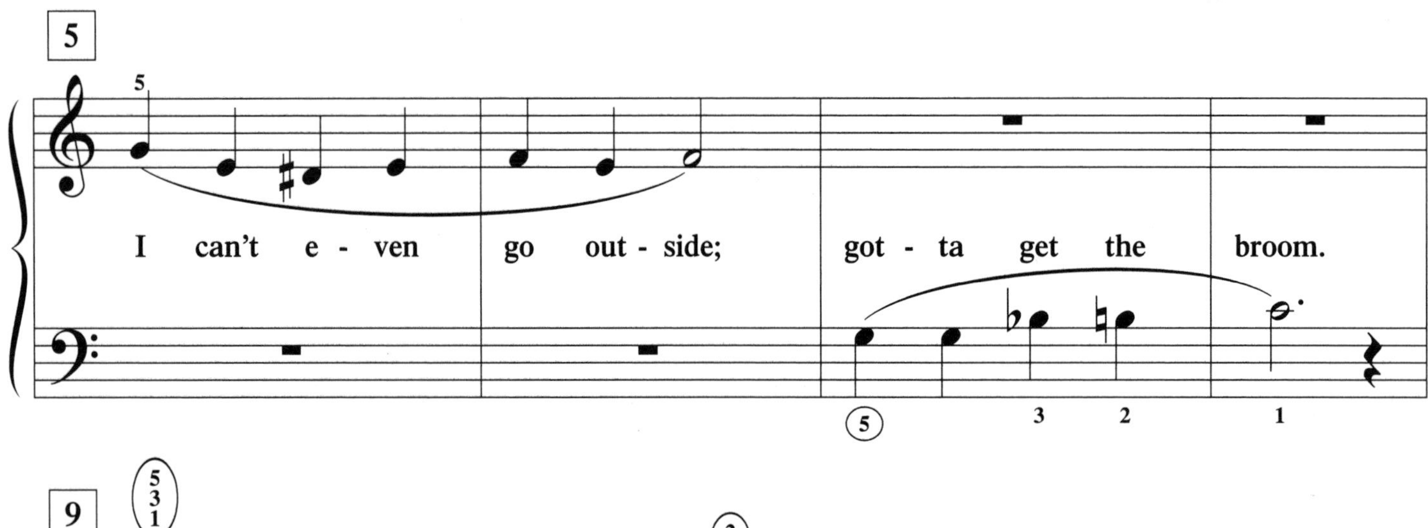

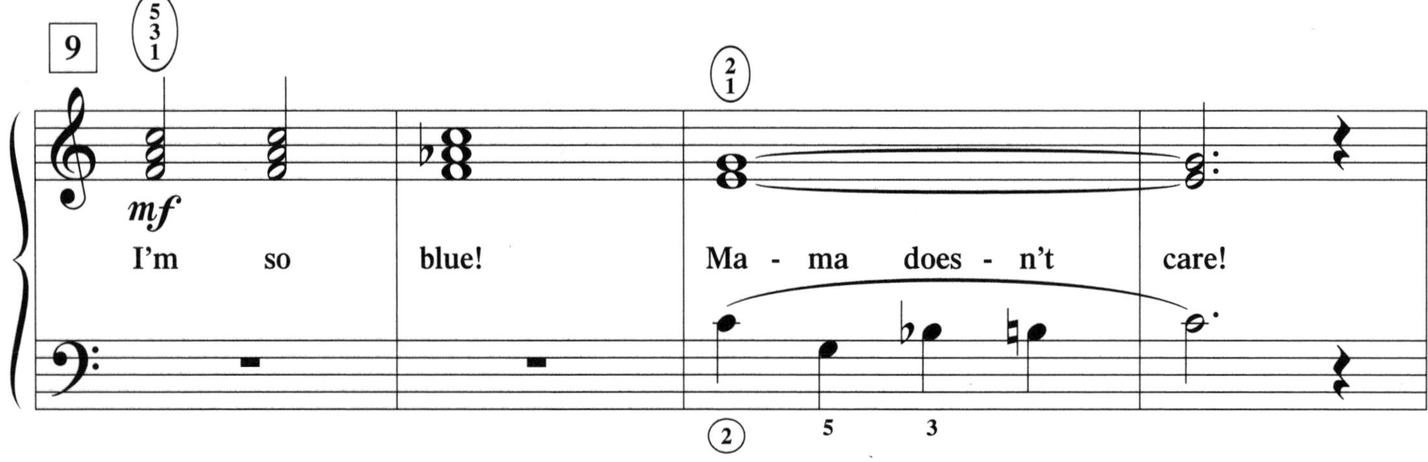

Teacher Duet: (Student plays 1 octave higher)

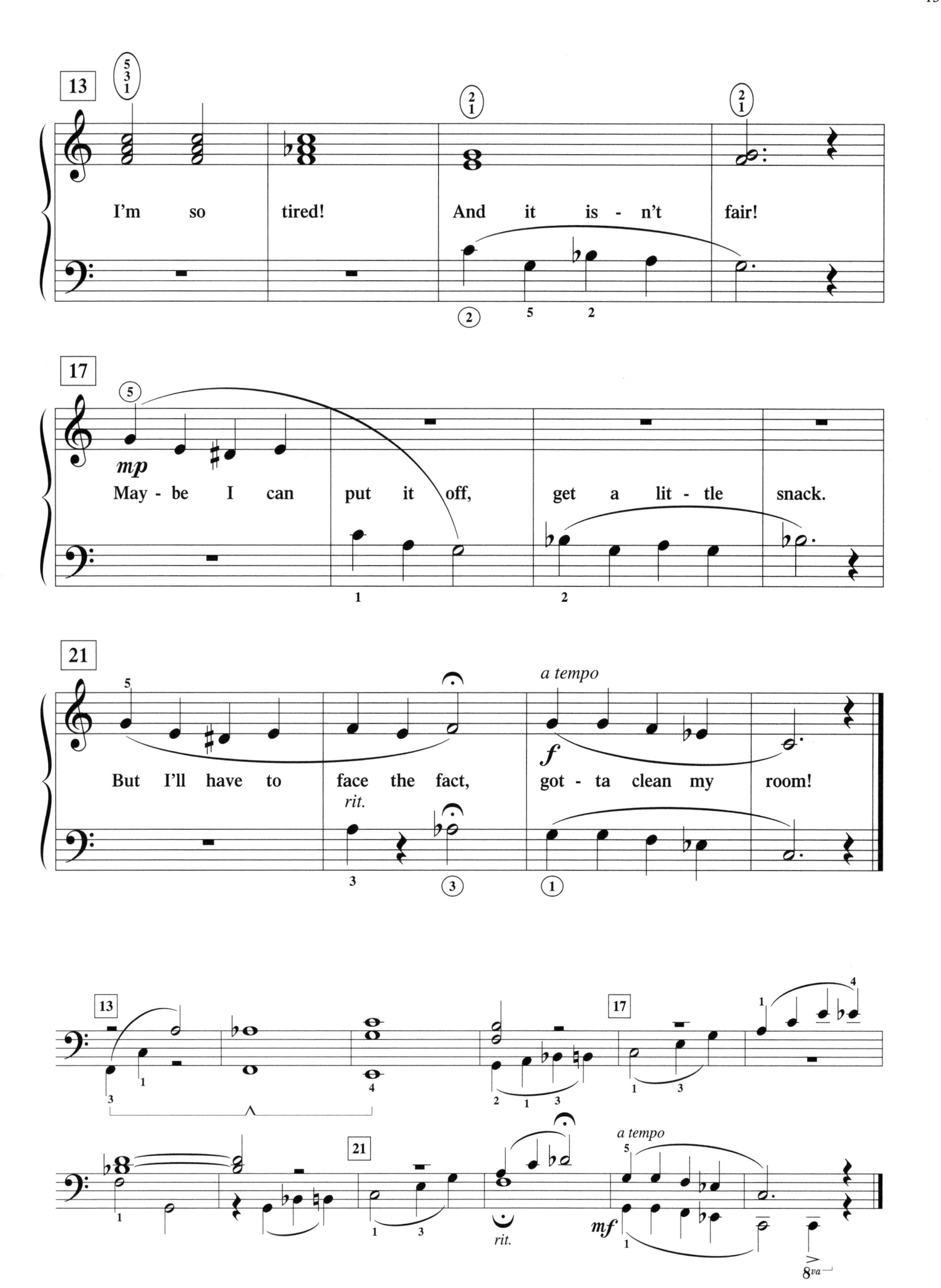
13
I'm so tired!
And it is - n't fair!
17
mp
May - be I can put it off, get a lit - tle snack.
21
a tempo
But I'll have to face the fact, got - ta clean my room!
rit.
f
13
17
21
a tempo
rit.
mf
8va

Ode to the Lima Bean

13
Ma - ma tried to bake it up, but now it's gone and
16
died.
mf
Poor old li - ma,
19
with - ered and a - lone;
Poor old li - ma,
23
dried up like a bone!
13
16
19
23

Rock Fever!

Fast and furious! 𝅗𝅥 = ca. 100

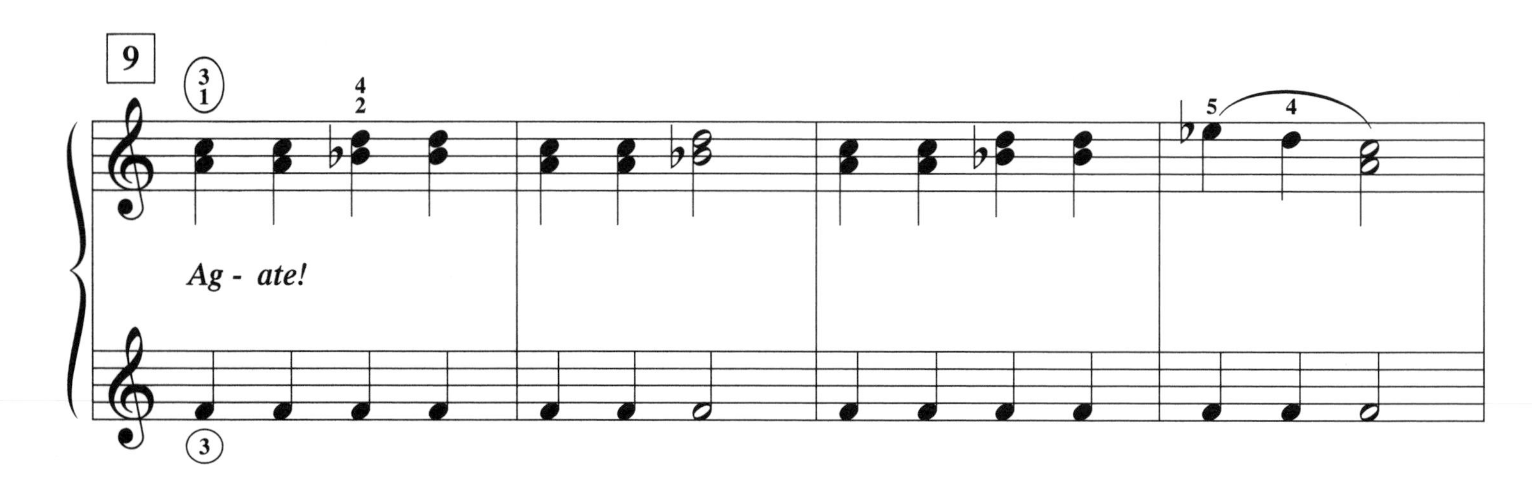

Teacher Duet: (Student plays 1 octave higher)

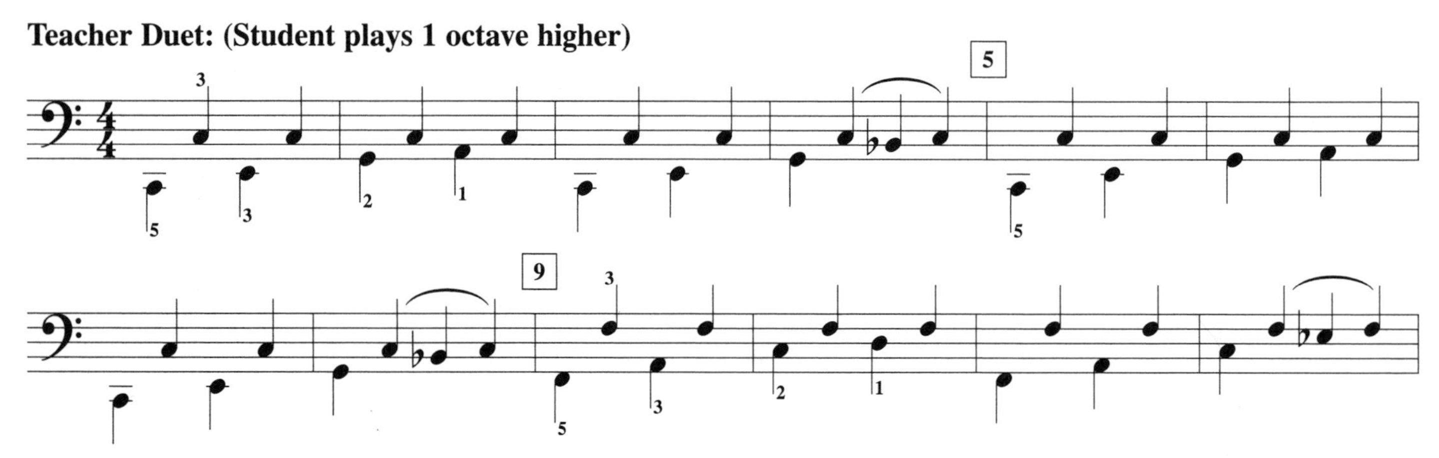

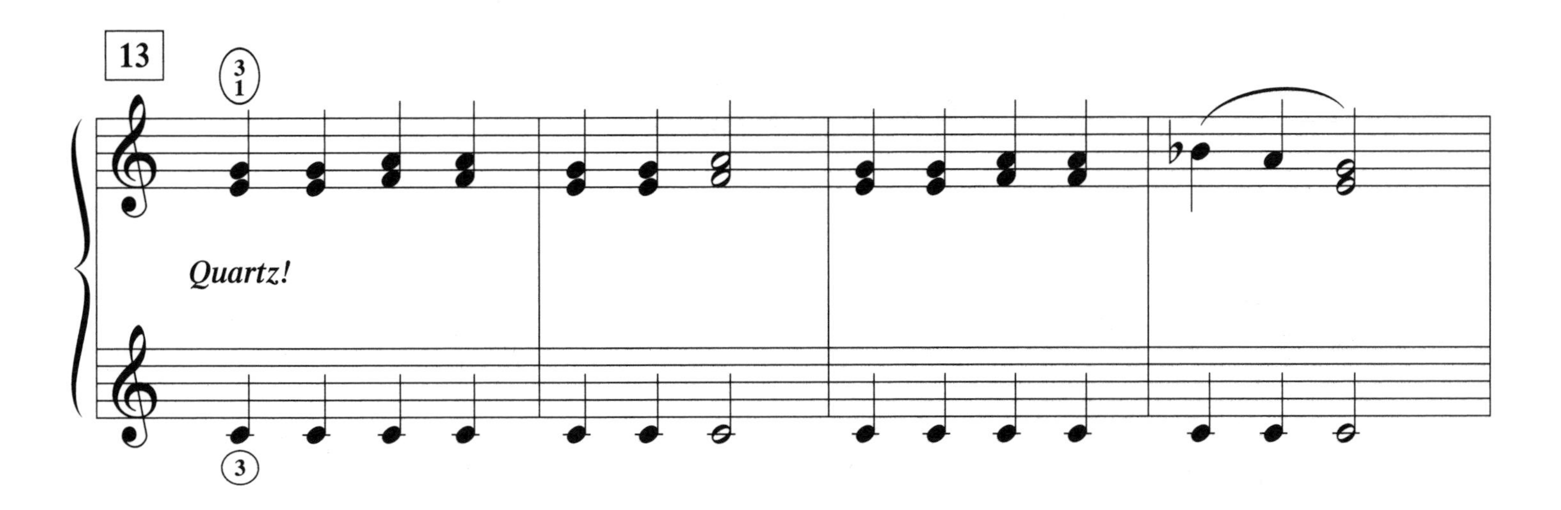
13
Quartz!

17
Dy - na - mite!
Kryp - to - nite!
Out of sight!
Me - teor - ite!

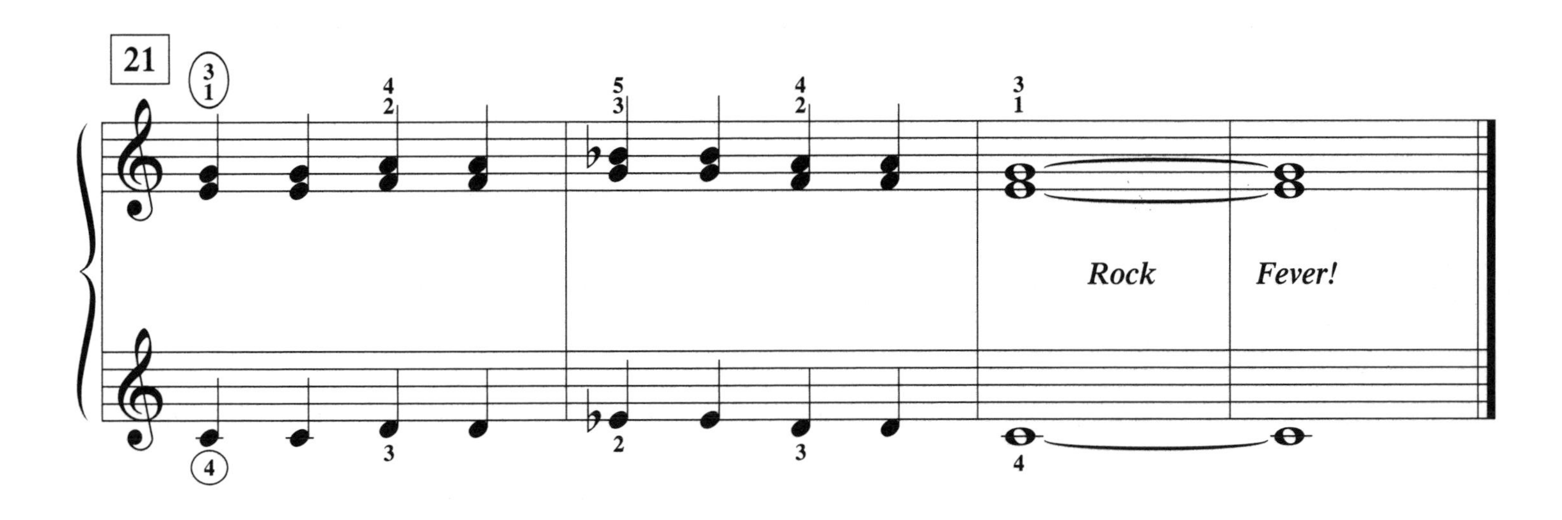
21
Rock
Fever!

13
17
21

Space Dreams

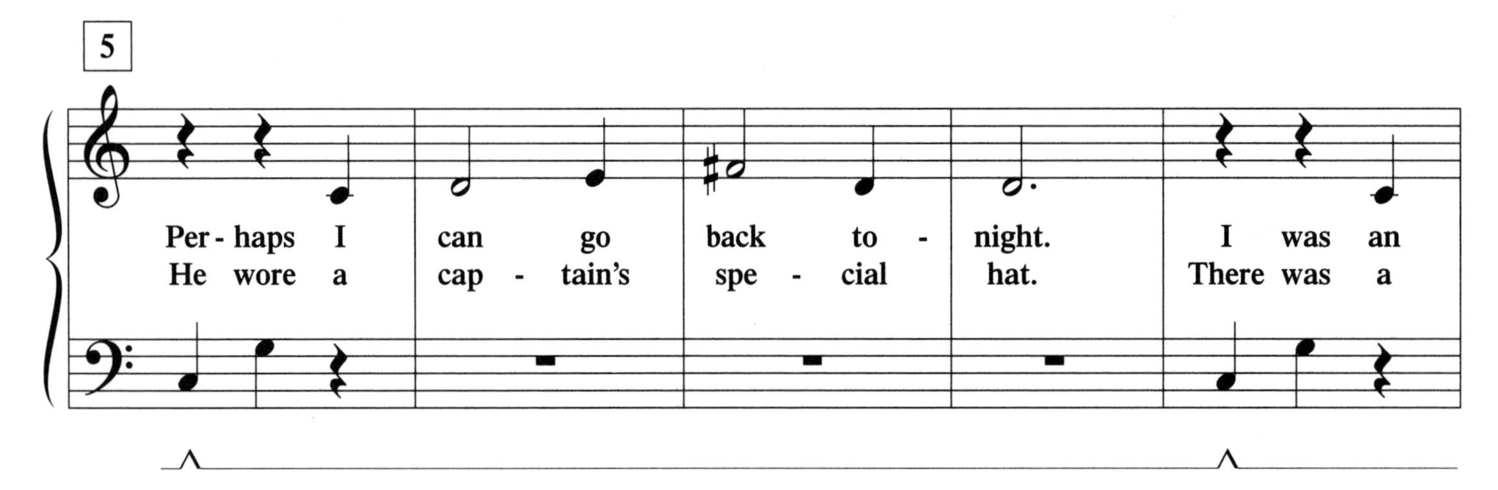

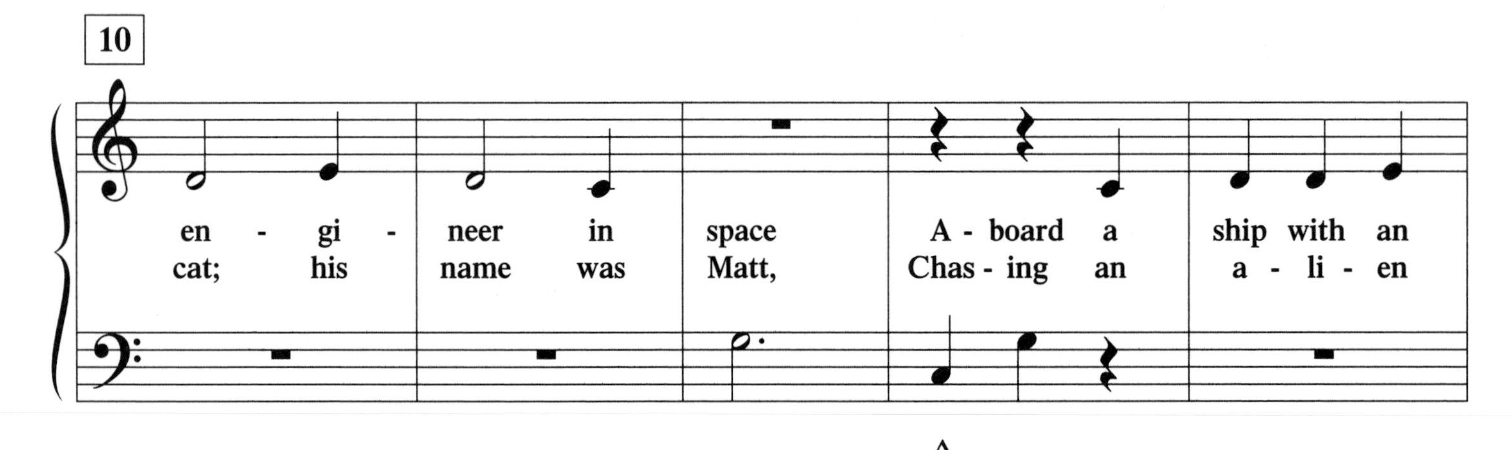

21
1
Ma - ma, she was the han - dy - man;
mp
5
25
She oiled all the dan - dy gears.
29
My dad, he float - ed up - side down
33
4
As he was slurp - ing a cos - mic root beer.
39
1
I was the chief com - man - der, and
mf
5

43
I told them what to do.
47
And if you dare, bet - ter be - ware!
p
mp
51
To-night I'll come and take you too!
mf
57
f
L.H.
R.H.
8va
L.H.
62
(8va)
R.H.
L.H.
Space
Dreams!